this coloring book belongs to

____

____

HAPPY

diwali

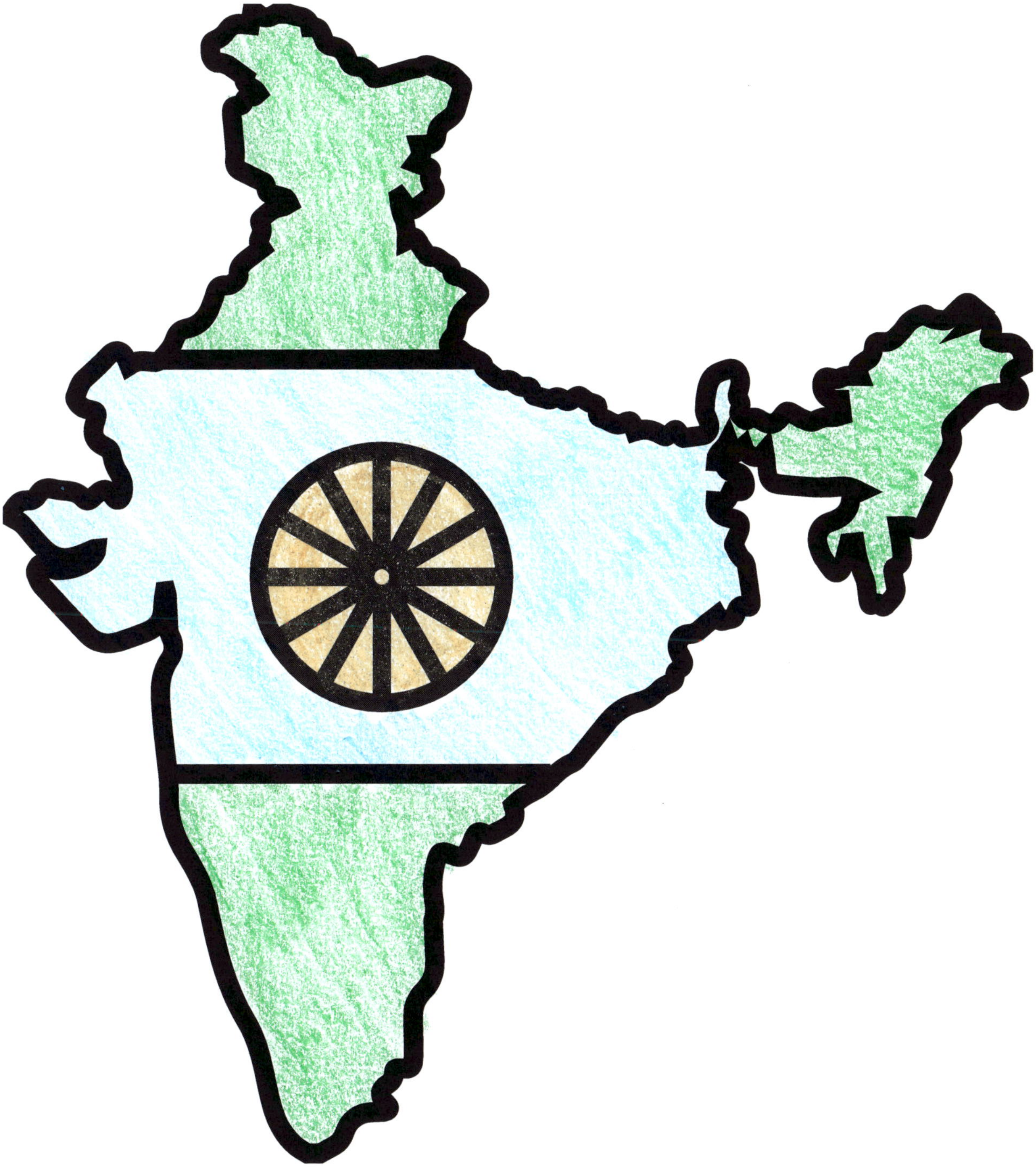

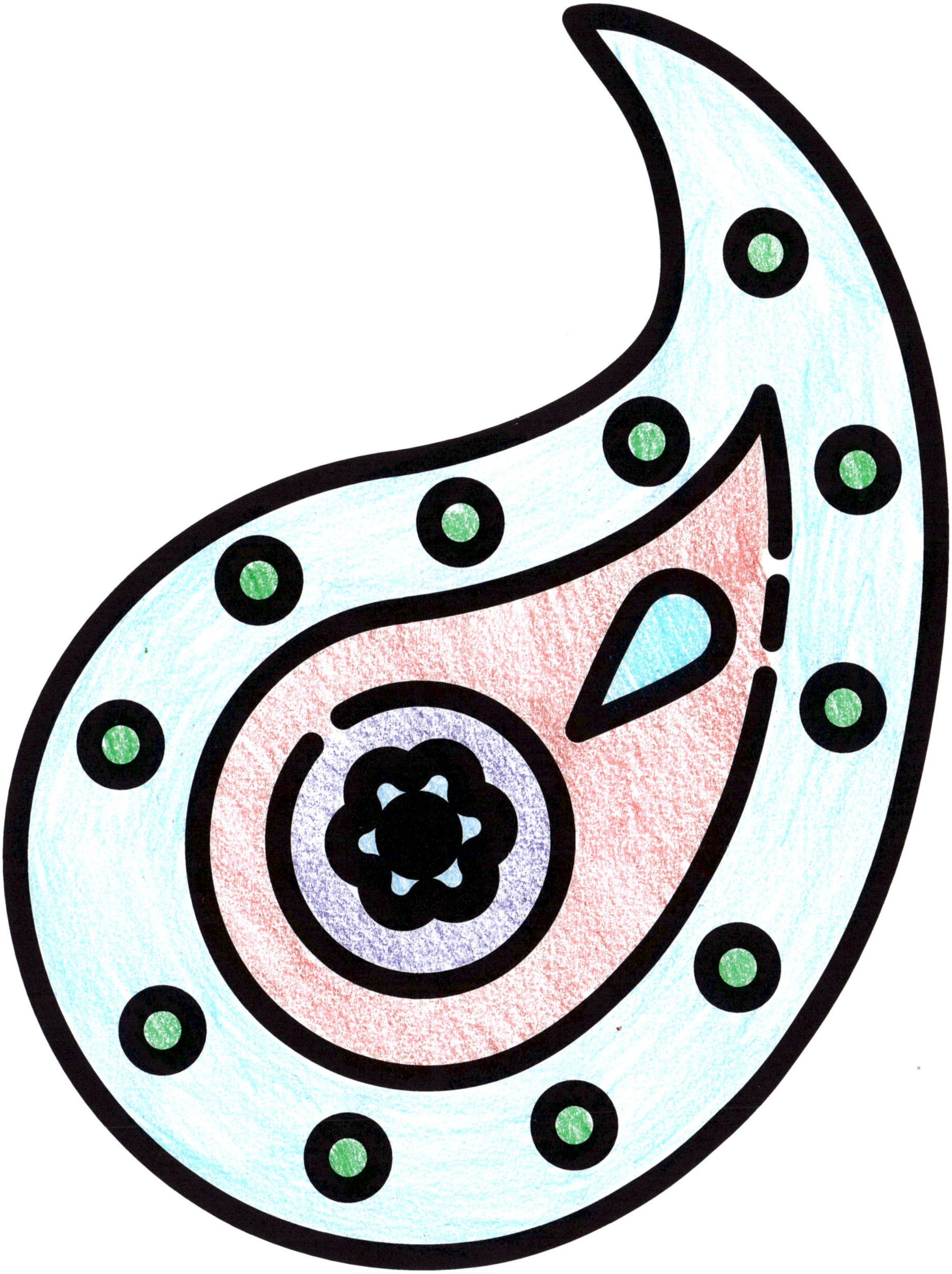

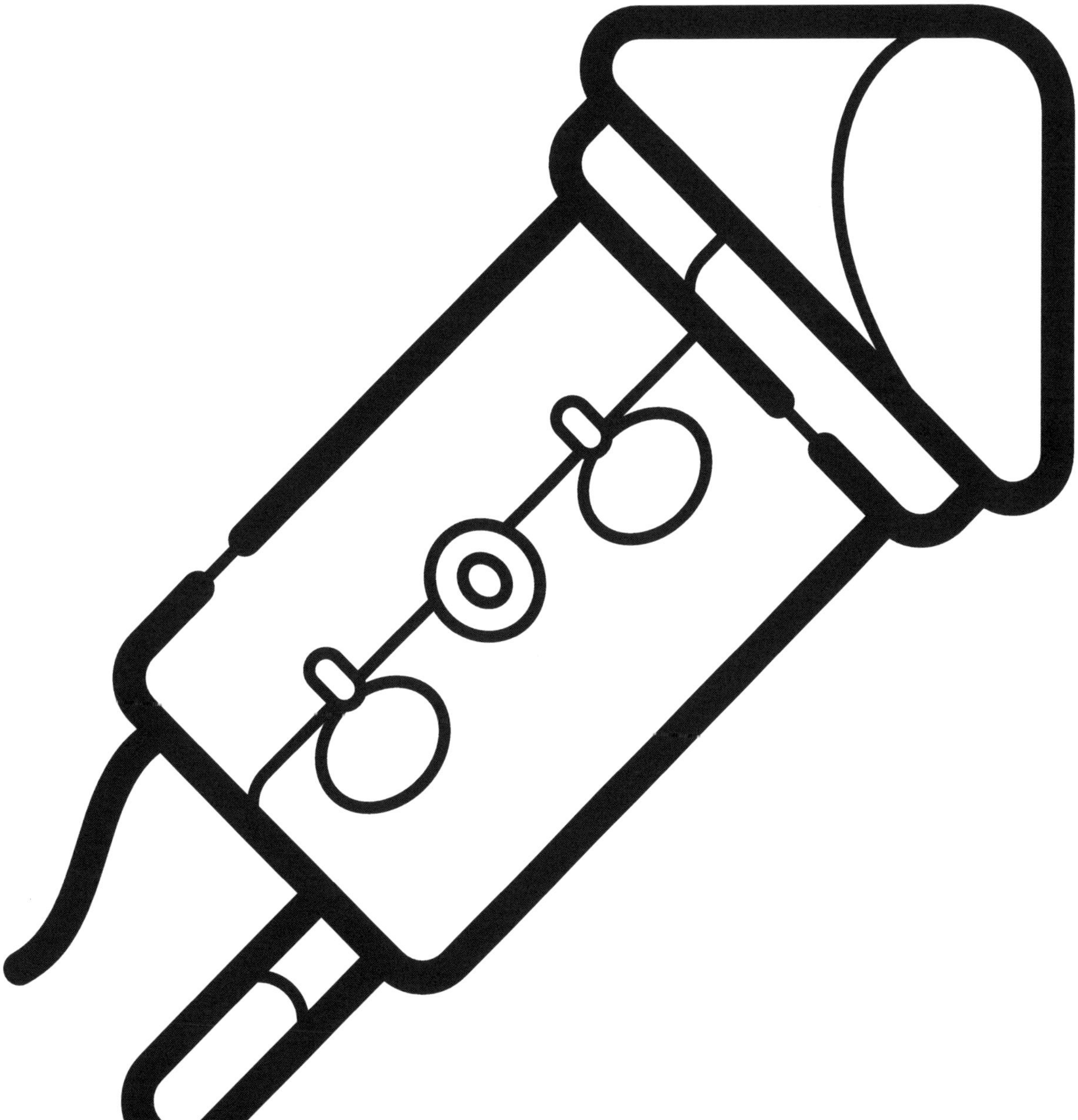

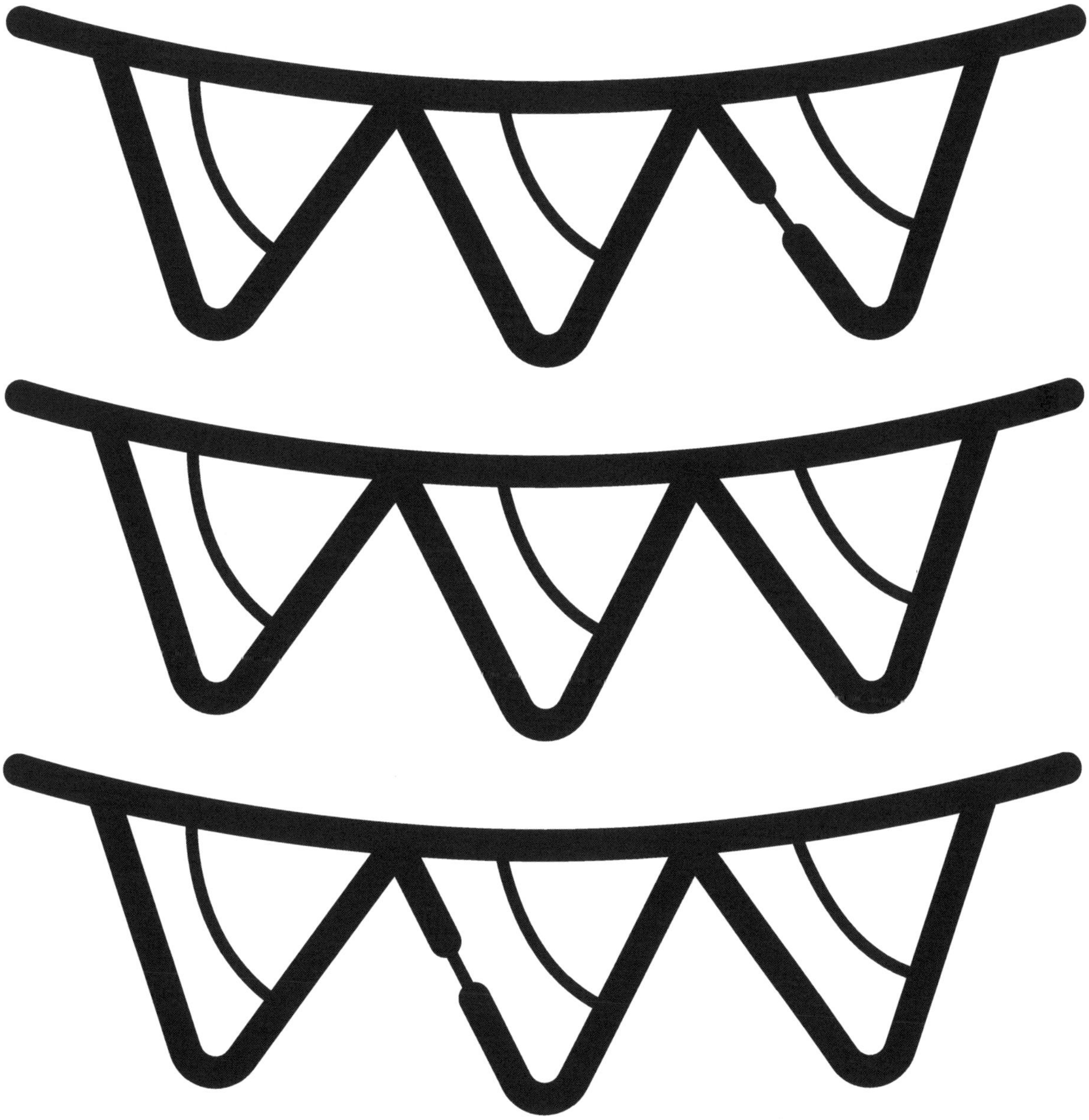

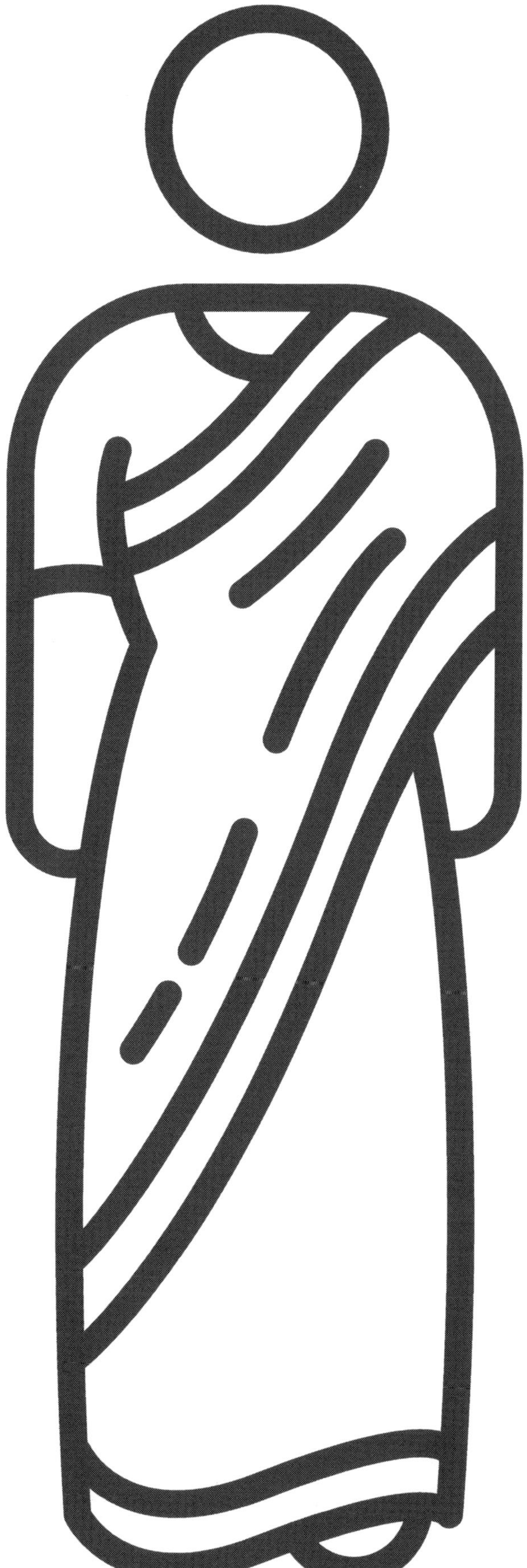

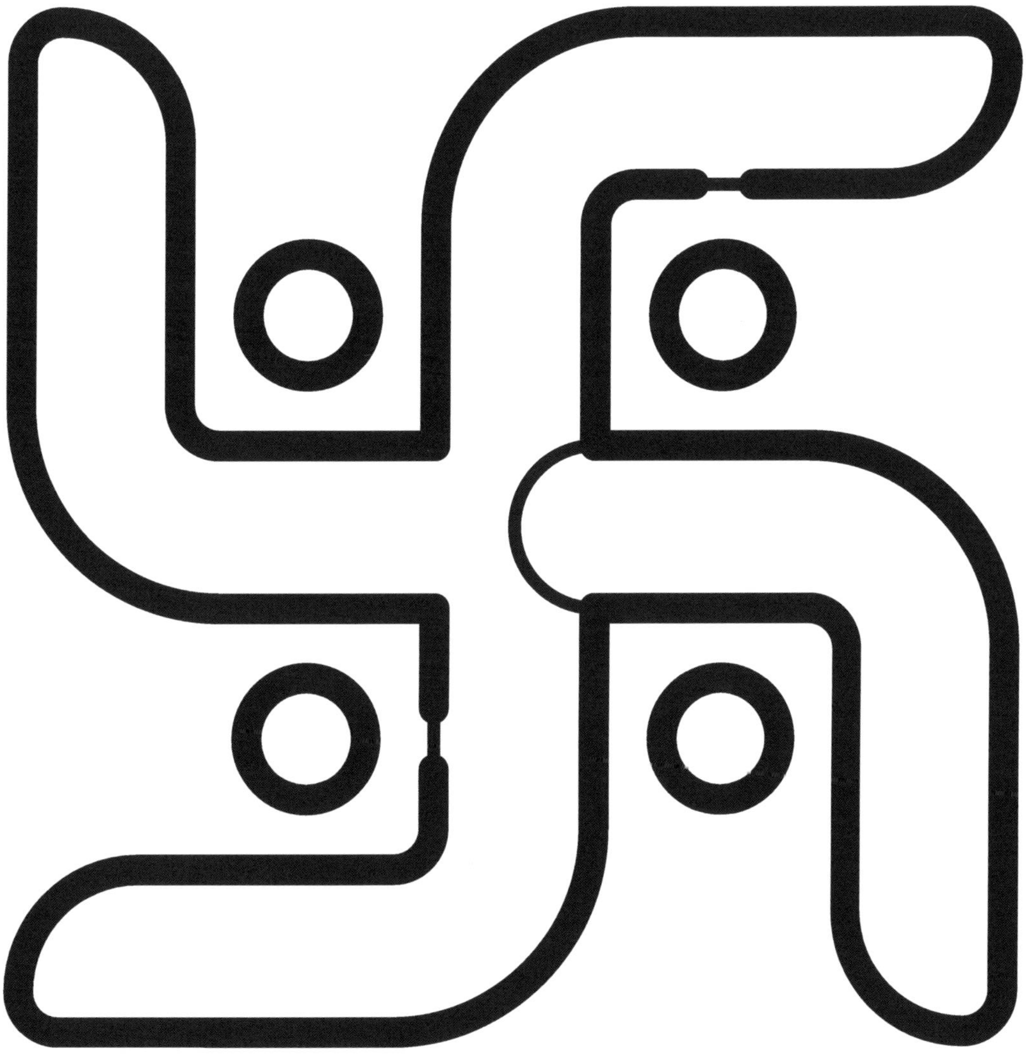

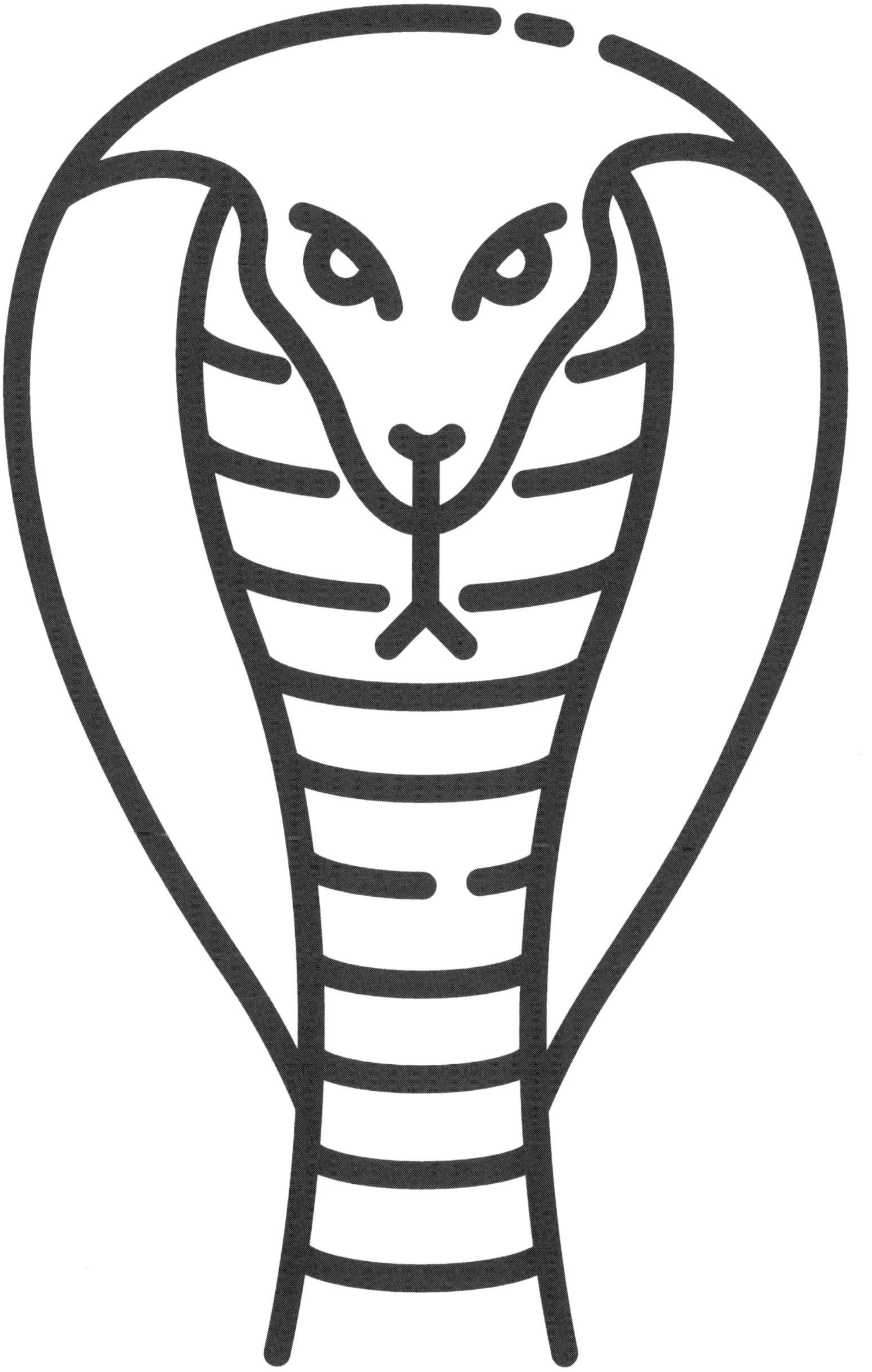

Made in the USA
Middletown, DE
13 December 2021

55421946R00057